NEEDLECRAFT

Susie O'Reilly

With photographs by Zul Mukhida

Thomson Learning

New York

Books in this series

BATIK AND TIE-DYE
BLOCK PRINTING
KNITTING AND CROCHET
MODELING
NEEDLECRAFT
PAPERMAKING
STENCILS AND SCREENS
WEAVING

Title page *Detail from a* mola,
*appliqué work of the Cuna Indians
of the San Blas Islands, off the coast
of Panama.*

First published in the
United States in 1994 by
Thomson Learning
115 Fifth Avenue
New York, NY 10003

Published simultaneously in
Great Britain by
Wayland (Publishers) Ltd.

U.K. copyright © 1994
Wayland (Publishers) Ltd.

U.S. copyright © 1994
Thomson Learning

Library of Congress Cataloging-in-Publication Data
O'Reilly, Susie, 1949-
    Needlecraft/Susie O'Reilly; with photographs by Zul Mukhida.
        p.   cm.—(Arts & crafts)
    Includes bibliographical references and index.
    ISBN 1-56847-220-X
    1. Needlework—Juvenile literature. [1. Needlework.] I. Mukhida,
Zul, ill. II. Title. III. Series: O'Reilly, Susie, 1949– Arts & crafts.
TT712.074   1994
746.4—dc20   94-12264

Printed in Italy

CONTENTS

Words printed in **bold** appear in the glossary.

GETTING STARTED

This book explores some of the many ways in which a simple needle and thread can be used to create wonderful art and craftwork. All kinds of different **fibers** and **fabrics** can be used. For example paper, plastic, and leather can be used as thread to sew with – or they can form the background material used for sewing on. Found and recycled objects can be added to the work. Dyed, printed, and painted cloth can be used as the background for a piece of work or sewn onto other fabrics.

Embroidering ▶ *by hand is a slow job.*

▼ *The richly decorated surface of this piece was created by adding lots of buttons to the embroidered designs.*

In the past, one of the main ways of judging sewn and **embroidered** work was the neatness and accuracy of the stitching. Now, it is no longer so important for the **wrong side** to be as neat as the right side of the work. What is important is for the piece to be exciting and interesting to look at, and that it communicate an idea or feeling to the person looking at it.

◀ *This hand-embroidered pillowcase was made in northern India.*

SETTING UP YOUR WORK AREA

You will need to collect these tools and materials to get started.

Fabrics and materials
Try to find a wide range of different materials: cloth; plastic; leather; paper; plain and patterned fabrics (for example, tie-dyed, batik, and block printed cloth); fabrics of different weights and **textures**; **burlap** or **canvas**.

Threads
For example: cotton thread; embroidery threads; yarn; tapestry yarns; string; strips of leather; strips of paper; thin wire.

Found objects
Look for objects to glue or sew on: beads; buttons; bottle tops; pebbles; sequins; scraps of colored paper; scraps of metal.

Needles
Crewel needles (slim, pointed needles with narrow **eyes** for plain sewing)
Chenille needles (broad, pointed needles with wide eyes for thick threads)
Beading needles (extremely fine, long needles with narrow eyes)
Tapestry needles (broad needles with blunt ends and wide eyes for canvas work)

Other equipment
Steel pins
Sharp fabric scissors
Pinking shears
An embroidery hoop or frame (or an old picture frame and thumbtacks)
HeatnBond
Wonder-Under
Iron
Ironing board
Ruler
Set square
Tape measure
All-purpose scissors
Soft pencil
Fabric glue
Squared paper
Rough paper
Camera
Notebook
Colored markers or crayons

THE HISTORY OF SEWING

We can only guess when, and how, people first started to use a needle and thread to join pieces of cloth together. Evidence from ancient paintings, documents, and stories suggests that people have been sewing and embroidering since earliest times. But unlike clay, wood, or metal, cloth does not last a long time. If it gets wet or is left in the light, it wears out and disintegrates. As a result, few examples of sewn and embroidered work made before the tenth century survive today.

In the beginning, people probably experimented with ways of joining pieces of animal skin and tree bark, using pieces of vegetable fiber or

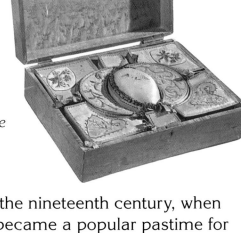

This American needlework box is over 200 years old. ▶

◀ *This bone needle and case dates back to before 4000 BC.*

animal gut. Needles, made of bone or horn, have been used for at least 20,000 years. Pins may have been made from fish bones. Iron needles, with a hook instead of an eye to hold the thread, were used in the fourteenth century. The first needles with eyes, it seems, were made in Egypt in 4000 B.C. or before.

Over the centuries, all the tools that are now used to cut, sew, and decorate fabric developed. The ancient Romans used sprung shears, rather like sheep shears. They also used scissors with **pivoted** blades similar to those used today.

In Europe in the nineteenth century, when needlework became a popular pastime for wealthy women, people made wonderfully elaborate pincushions, needle cases, and work boxes.

People have always wanted to decorate their fabrics with embroidery stitches or by sewing on eye-catching objects such as jewels, shells, beads, and scraps of glass and metal. These fabrics were very important to the **societies** that produced them. They indicated a person's power or wealth and were used to celebrate major events such as weddings and funerals.

◄ A crazy-quilted door curtain made in 1887.

Making silk brocade in Varanasi, India. ▼

It is easy for us to think of needlecraft as women's work. But across all centuries and all societies, both men and women have developed needlecraft skills. Generally speaking, men are more noted for their skill as **tailors**, but this is not always the case. In India, the most advanced embroidery has traditionally been done by male embroiderers. Even today, it is the men who make the highly decorated **cashmere** shawls and produce elaborate gold and silver thread work. In England in the thirteenth and fourteenth centuries, and again in the sixteenth century, embroidery was considered a man's job.

Some sewing techniques arose from a particular need. In **medieval** Europe, quilting was used to make warm bedclothes. Medieval knights also wore quilted clothing as padding under their armor. Patchwork was necessary at times when fabric was scarce. Leftover snippets of cloth, or pieces cut from old, worn clothes, were sewn together to make new items.

Later, sewing was not just a useful skill, it was also a way of showing off. In the eighteenth and nineteenth centuries, in Europe and North America, women and girls produced beautiful embroidered **samplers** using tiny, perfect stitches.

In western countries, artists are exploring the traditions of sewing and embroidery. Many have been trained as painters and use a needle and thread on fabric just as they might use a brush and paint.

◄ This sampler was made using cotton with silk threads.

Louise ► Baldwin used paper as a base for this piece, which she backed with felt.

TECHNIQUES AROUND THE WORLD

The idea of using needlework to paint a picture or tell a story has been around for centuries. Perhaps the most famous example is the Bayeux Tapestry, made in the eleventh or twelfth century in France. It is in fact not a tapestry at all (the word "tapestry" usually means a piece of weaving), but a huge embroidery, using colorful woolen threads on a linen background. It tells the story of the Norman king, William the Conqueror, who conquered England in 1066, and contains a series of different scenes.

In the eighteenth and nineteenth centuries, particularly in North America, embroidered portraits were popular. George Washington, the first President of the United States (1789-1797), was a common subject.

◀ *Queen Elizabeth I favored dresses embroidered with fine threads.*

▲ *A scene from the Bayeux Tapestry.*

A very fancy kind of embroidery uses metal thread to add extra sparkle. This technique has a long tradition in China and other parts of the Far East. In Europe, kings and queens wore clothes beautifully decorated with metal thread and jewels. Portraits of Queen Elizabeth I of England (1558-1603) show her wearing spectacular embroidered dresses.

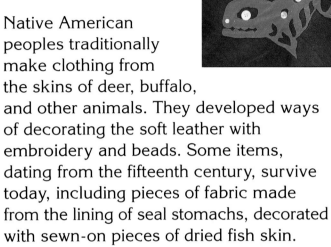

◀ A piece of embroidery from northern India.

A Haida Indian making and wearing a button blanket. ▶

Appliqué is the technique of sewing pieces of fabric onto a backing cloth to make a picture or design. Many different societies around the world have traditions of using appliqué. Embroidery stitches and extra objects – buttons, tinkling bells, or scraps of metal, for example – may be sewn on for color, decoration, or to add a special meaning. In the dry deserts of northern India and Afghanistan, where water is very important, pieces of sparkling glass are sewn onto cloth to look like the sun glinting on water.

Native American peoples traditionally make clothing from the skins of deer, buffalo, and other animals. They developed ways of decorating the soft leather with embroidery and beads. Some items, dating from the fifteenth century, survive today, including pieces of fabric made from the lining of seal stomachs, decorated with sewn-on pieces of dried fish skin.

From the sixteenth century on, Europeans started to settle in the Americas. In North America, people developed a tradition of making bed quilts, using a combination of patchwork, quilting, and appliqué. Making a quilt was a sociable affair. The women of a village would gather at a "quilting bee" to make a quilt to celebrate a birth or a twenty-first birthday or to mourn a death. Some of the quilts were made from whole pieces of cloth. Others were pieced together using small shapes of cloth, to make a dazzling patchwork design. Some of the traditional designs have colorful names referring to events of the time, such as "Rocky Road to California," "Texas Tears," and "Kansas Troubles."

◀ A floral design quilt made by a "quilting bee" in the United States in the 1800s.

SOME BASIC TECHNIQUES

CUTTING OUT

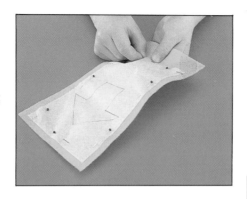

1 Iron your piece of fabric flat. It helps to dampen the cloth by spraying it with water. Use a plant sprayer to do this. **Ask an adult to help you with the iron.**

2 Mark the shapes of the pieces you want to cut on the fabric. You can do this by pinning paper shapes (**patterns**) to the fabric or by using a piece of chalk. With chalk, the lines can easily be brushed off and will not spoil the finished work.

3 Cut the fabric using sharp scissors. Try to keep a special pair of scissors just for fabric. Don't use them to cut paper as well – paper will blunt the scissors.

KEEPING FABRIC FROM FRAYING

The edges of some fabrics **fray** easily. Here are several ways you can avoid frayed edges.

1 Choose fabrics that have been very tightly woven, so that they will not unravel.

2 Work with pieces of nonwoven material, such as plastic, leather, or felt.

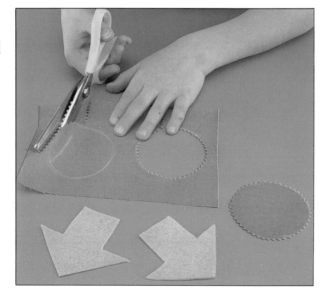

3 Use pinking shears to cut the fabric. The zigzag or scalloped edge made by pinking shears does not fray as easily as the straight edge made by ordinary scissors.

4 Buy a nonfraying cloth, such as iron-on HeatnBond or Wonder-Under, which can be ironed onto the back of your fabric before you start cutting. Place the sticky side down on the back of your fabric and pass a cool iron over it to make it stick. **Ask an adult to help you with the iron**.

MAKING A HEM

A hem is an edge of fabric that has been folded over several times and stitched down to keep the fabric from fraying.

1 Lay your work out flat, with the wrong side up.

2 Press it using a cool iron and a damp cloth. **Ask an adult to help you with the iron.**

3 Turn under a 3/4-inch edge. Iron it flat.

4 Turn the edge under again another 3/4 inch. Iron it flat.

5 Use pins or **tacking** stitches to hold the hem in place.

6 Use tiny hemming stitches to sew the hem down. Pick up just a few threads of fabric where the stitch will show through on the right side, and then catch the folded edge with a bigger stitch.

7 If you like, use a decorative stitch, such as a blanket stitch, herringbone stitch, or feather stitch, to make a feature of the edging.

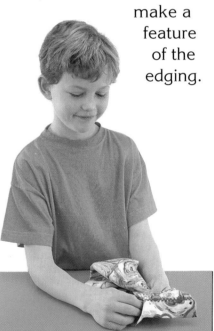

TURN TO PAGES 12-15 FOR INFORMATION ON STITCHES.

MAKING STITCHES

There are hundreds of different stitches. Start by learning some of the basic stitches needed to join pieces of fabric together. Then experiment, using different sizes of stitches, placing the stitches close together or far apart, and using different thicknesses of thread. In this way, you can make a range of different designs. Make a stitched sampler to remind you of your ideas.

All stitches belong to one of four basic groups: flat, looped, crossed, and knotted stitches.

FLAT STITCHES

Flat stitches are worked on the surface of the fabric. These are the easiest of all stitches and are found in the world's earliest known embroideries.

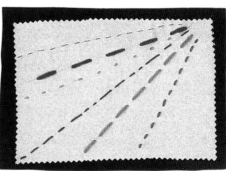

1 Running stitch

This is the basic stitch for hand sewing. In embroidery, it is used to make lines and outlines, and as a basis for other stitches. Running stitches are often used to tack pieces of fabric together firmly while they are being worked on. The tacking stitches are removed once the real sewing has been completed. To make running stitches, simply pass the needle in and out of the fabric in a line.

2 Variations on running stitch

A running stitch usually has small, neat stitches, the same size on the right and wrong side of the fabric. Try making the right-side stitches huge and the wrong-side ones tiny. Make some stitches on the right side long and others short. Experiment using thick and thin thread. Try making all the stitches **horizontal**. Then make them all **vertical**.

3 Straight stitch

Bring the needle up to the right side of the cloth and then down again. The stitches can be arranged in lines, circles, or any way you like.

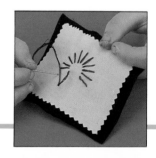

4 Satin stitch

These flat stitches of varying lengths are stitched very close together to fill areas of work with color.

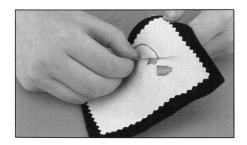

5 Stem stitch

This stitch can be used in many different ways: for backgrounds, fillings, lines, and outlines. Holding the thread down on the right side of the fabric and to the side of the needle, make a

6 Hemming stitch

stitch by bringing the needle back to the right side of the fabric through the hole made by the previous stitch.

This is useful for making invisible stitches and hems. Catch the folded-over hem, picking up just a few threads of fabric where the stitch will show through to the right side.

CROSSED STITCHES

These are formed with two or more stitches, which can cross each other in a variety of different ways. Cross stitch is one of the oldest known of all embroidery stitches. It was widely used by the ancient Egyptians. Traditional embroideries of many countries use cross stitch a great deal.

bottom left-hand corner and make the "cross" stitch. Take the needle to start the next stitch in the top left-hand corner. The stitches should always pass in the same direction unless you want to make a special effect of light and shade.

2 Half-cross stitch

This is also known as the tent stitch. It is often used in embroideries that are designed on a grid (see pages 16-17). Make a diagonal stitch from top left to bottom right. Take the needle to the top right-hand corner and make a diagonal stitch **parallel** to the first. For the second row, work from right to left, making the stitches from bottom right to top left. The top of the stitches will use

the same holes as the bottom of the first row of stitches.

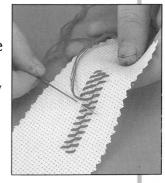

3 Herringbone stitch

This can be used instead of a blanket stitch as a decorative hemming or edging stitch. Make a fairly long diagonal stitch. Bring the needle back through the fabric, at the same height, but a little way back along the stitch. Make a diagonal stitch in the other direction and again bring the needle back a little way to start the next stitch.

1 Cross stitch

Make a **diagonal** stitch from top left to bottom right. Take the needle to the

LOOPED STITCHES

These are made by the thread being looped on the surface of the fabric and held down with a stitch.

1 Chain stitch

The chain stitch is ideal for making decorative lines of stitches, or it can be used instead of satin stitch to fill in areas with color. Bring the needle through to the right side of the fabric. Hold the thread down with your thumb. Take the needle down through the same hole and then back up through to the right side of the fabric, about 1/3 inch away. Repeat to make a line of stitches.

2 Blanket stitch

This is a very useful hemming and edging stitch. It can be used to join two overlapping pieces of fabric together or to edge buttonholes. Hold a loop of thread from the previous

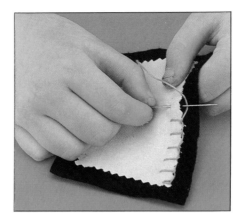

stitch and push the needle through from the right to the wrong side of the fabric, a little way in from the edge. Bring the needle back toward the edge of the fabric, catching the loop of thread.

3 Lazy daisy

Make in the same way as a single chain stitch. Catch the stitch in place by taking the needle over the looped thread and down through the fabric. These stitches sewn in a circle look like flower petals.

4 Fly stitch

This is also known as open loop. Mark the line the stitching will follow. Bring the needle through to the right side of the fabric. Take the thread across the cloth as if you were making a straight stitch. Before you pull it flat, bring the needle up in the middle of the line of the stitching lower down and catch the thread. The "stalk" of the Y can be as long or as short as you like.

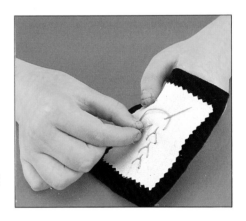

5 Feather stitch

This is a light, delicate stitch, which can be used for filling, edging, and holding overlapping pieces of fabric. Mark the line the stitching will follow. Push the needle through to the right side of the fabric. Hold the thread diagonally across the line and make a small diagonal stitch back

toward the line, catching the loop of thread. Repeat on the other side.

Some of the patterns and designs you can create using the different stitches described here. Can you figure out which stitches have been used? ▶

KNOTTED STITCHES

These are formed by knotting or twisting the thread on the surface of the fabric and securing the knot with a stitch.

French knots

These can be dotted over an area to give the effect of a light smattering of color. They can also be worked closely together to build up an area of textured color. Bring the needle through to the right side of the fabric. Twist the needle several times around the thread, and take it back down through the same hole in the fabric.

OTHER STITCHES

1 Couching

Couching enables objects and unusual fibers, which may be too delicate or too bulky to be sewn in and out of the fabric, to be attached to work. Place the object or piece of fiber on the fabric and use small stitches to catch it in place. To make a bolder effect, try couching several fibers side by side.

2 Combinations

All the stitches described so far can be combined with one another to make raised effects or to create bolder and more decorative designs. Experiment with different ideas.

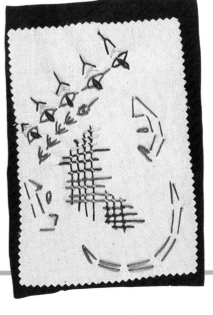

USING A GRID

Many fabrics are woven using a **loom** to interlace vertical threads with horizontal threads. Some fabrics, such as burlap and needlepoint canvas, are very loosely woven and the **grid** made by the interlaced threads can be used as a framework for an embroidered design. Either the half-cross (tent) stitch or cross stitch is used to completely cover the fabric with thread. Using the grid, the stitches can be sized and positioned evenly.

Embroideries made in this way are called needlepoint. They are extremely hard-wearing and are suitable for making into chair seats, cushions, bags, and purses.

1 Using graph paper, work out your design. Try to simplify shapes. Build up "steps" of blocked color rather than using curves.

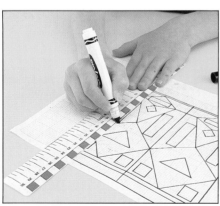

2 Cut out a piece of burlap or canvas. Allow at least 4 inches of extra fabric all around to make a border and for seams and hems.

3 Outline your main design on the fabric.

4 Thread a tapestry needle (the large eye and blunt point are ideal for needlepoint) with tapestry yarn.

5 Take the needle down through the canvas, leaving a loose end of thread on the top of the work. Then work your stitches over it so that the end is hidden and firmly secured. This gives a better result than tying a knot in the thread.

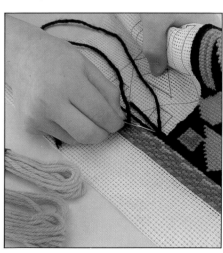

BASIC TECHNIQUES

6 Work half-cross stitches in rows, from left to right and then from right to left, to fill in the blocks of color. When you have finished an area of color, cut the thread, leaving a loose end at the back of the work. Thread the loose end into the back of the other stitches.

TURN TO PAGE 13 FOR INFORMATION ON HALF-CROSS STITCH.

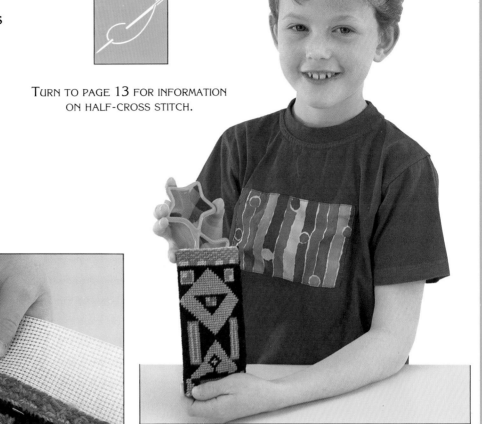

10 Fold the needlepoint in half and sew up the bottom and side.

7 When you have filled in all the areas of color, use a damp cloth and a cool iron and press the work on the wrong side. **Ask an adult to help you with the iron**.

8 To make the eyeglass case shown on this page, make a lining. Cut out a piece of lining fabric, half an inch bigger all around than your needlepoint.

9 With the two wrong sides together, tuck in the edge of the lining and sew it in place with tiny hemming stitches.

17

APPLIQUÉ

This technique involves sewing pieces of fabric and small objects onto a piece of backing cloth to make a picture or a design. Embroidery stitches are often used to add extra color, detail, and decoration.

3 Look through your collection of fabrics and pick out pieces that have the right color, texture, and pattern for your design. You might want to look for **motifs** printed on the fabric, to cut out and recycle into your own work. Choose a fabric that will not fray.

1 Decide on a picture or design.

2 Find a suitable piece of fabric for the background. A firmly woven piece of cotton fabric would be a good choice.

4 Cut out the shapes you want.

5 Place the pieces on your background. Move them around until you are satisfied with the result.

6 Sew or glue the pieces onto the background fabric. If you use glue, choose a fabric glue or white glue. These are transparent when dry. If you sew on the pieces, use a simple running stitch as a tacking stitch to hold the pieces in place.

7 Add detail and color using embroidery or by sewing on other objects.

TURN TO PAGES 12-15 FOR INFORMATION ON STITCHES.

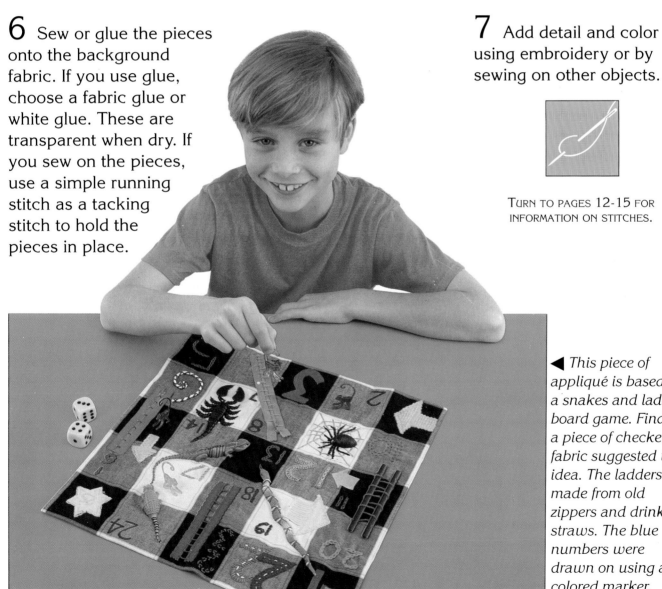

◄ *This piece of appliqué is based on a snakes and ladders board game. Finding a piece of checkered fabric suggested the idea. The ladders are made from old zippers and drinking straws. The blue numbers were drawn on using a colored marker.*

CRAZY QUILTING

For about twenty years, during the mid- to late nineteeneth century, crazy quilting was in fashion in Europe and the United States. Small scraps of rich, beautiful fabrics – silks, satins, velvets, **brocades**, brightly colored or printed cottons – were overlapped and stitched to a piece of backing fabric, in an apparently disordered way. Of course, in order to get a rich, detailed effect, careful thought and planning was needed.

Crazy quilting is an ideal technique for making small items such as cushion covers or small quilts for a baby carriage. If you want to make something bigger, such as a blanket or a curtain like the one shown on page 7, get a group of friends together and work as a team.

1 Select a piece of firmly woven fabric as your backing. Iron it carefully. Cover it with a piece of Wonder-Under. This is an artifical fabric which, when a warm iron is passed over it, sticks to other fabrics. **Ask an adult to help you with the iron**.

2 Look through your collection of fabrics. Find pieces in the colors you want. For this quilt, warm red, rich blue, and patterned scraps of velvet and corduroy have been used.

3 Arrange the scraps on the backing fabric so that one piece fits next to another. Take time doing this. Trim the scraps to size as necessary. Work to get an arrangement that really pleases your eye.

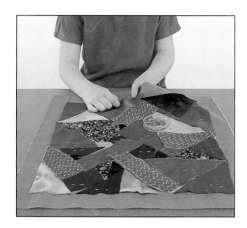

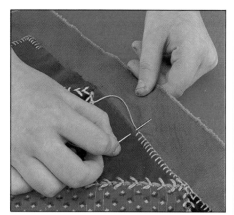

4
Once you are satisfied, pin the pieces in place. Place a damp cloth over it and iron it with a warm iron. The scraps will stick to the Wonder-Under. Remove the pins.

6
Choose an embroidery thread in a **contrasting** color (this piece uses golden yellow). Embroider the edges of the scraps with light, feathery stitches, such as the herringbone or feather stitch.

7
Blanket stitch all around the outside edges to finish off the piece.

TURN TO PAGES 12-15 FOR INFORMATION ON STITCHES.

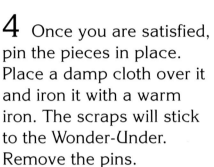

5
Using a piece of matching yarn, make large back stitches to fill in any gaps between the pieces.

TELLING A STORY

The Bayeux Tapestry (see page 8) tells the story of how the Normans, from northern France, conquered England in 1066. It includes lots of different scenes – French and English soldiers preparing for battle; pitched fighting; King Harold II of England falling off his horse and being killed.

Try telling your own story. You could use any of the different techniques explained in this book, such as embroidery, needlepoint, or appliqué. Choose a story that you have written yourself, a fairy tale, or a real event (something that has been in the news or something that has happened to you recently).

1 Look at ways of telling a story in pictures. Comic strips and cartoons in magazines and newspapers tell stories in a series of scenes. Look at pictures of medieval weavings and tapestries, or wall paintings from the thirteenth to sixteenth centuries telling stories from the Bible.

2 Decide on your story. Choose one that has a main character or characters who will appear in most of the scenes. These characters are repeating motifs and lead the viewer from scene to scene. It helps the viewer to understand that the work is a story that happens over a period of time.

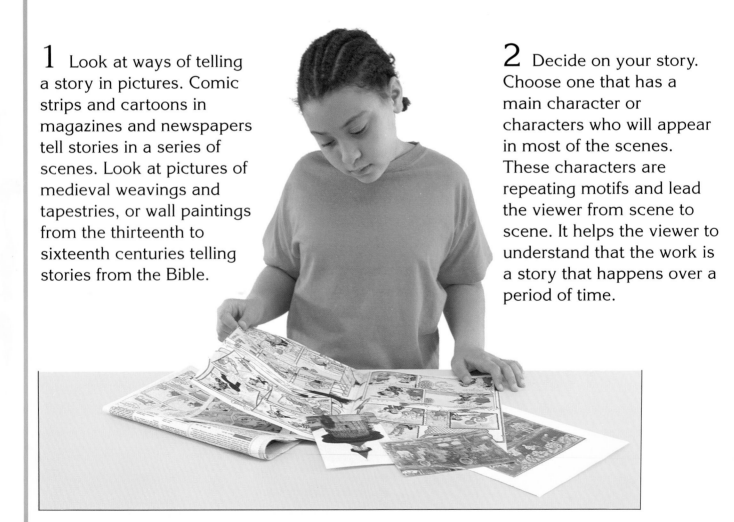

3 Decide which scenes from the story will be shown. Make drawings to help you plan the work – size, color combinations, techniques you will use, and materials you will need.

4 Get to work on making and sewing the piece. It will probably take quite a long time. You may decide to work with a group of friends. Each person could work on a part of the story and the pieces could be sewn together to make a quilt. To help the work along, hold a sewing bee, like colonial American quilters.

5 Cut out pieces of fabric for each scene.

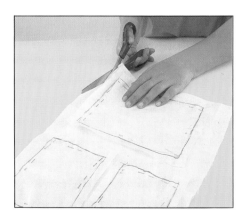

6 Arrange them on a piece of backing fabric to see how they will fit together.

7 Embroider each scene using various needlecraft techniques.

8 Sew the pieces to the backing fabric.

▼ *This piece shows two frogs getting married. Mr. Frog has a red bow tie. His bride has a red necklace. The rainbow shows them living happily ever after. Their "words" are in speech bubbles – just like in a comic strip.*

MAKING A FABRIC BOOK

All sorts of books are made of fabric. For example, there are cloth books for children who are too young to handle paper books; needle cases and pincushions are sometimes made in the shape of books. Make a fabric book in which to keep samples of embroidery stitches, or bind together **swatches** of different colors to make a book of sample fabrics.

1 Look carefully at some books, pamphlets, and magazines. Notice various features: the way the covers may be lined with endpapers; the position of the title; the way the pages are sewn or stapled together. Use this information to help you design your fabric book.

2 Decide on the size of the book and the number of pages.

3 Cut pieces of fabric for the pages. Each piece needs to be twice as wide as a single page. Choose fabric that will not fray, or use pinking shears. Or, line each page with another piece of fabric – fold over the edges and sew with running or hemming stitches.

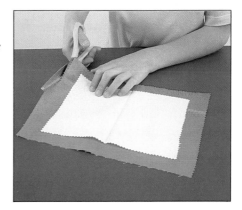

4 Fold the pages in half and iron in the central crease. **Ask an adult to help you with the iron**.

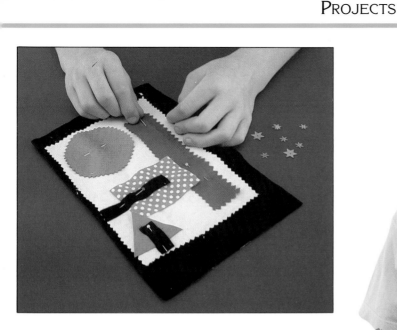

5 Make the outside cover using a hard-wearing fabric. Make it slightly larger than the inside pages. Use any of the techniques in this book to sew and decorate the cover.

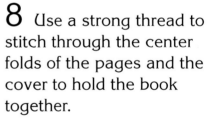

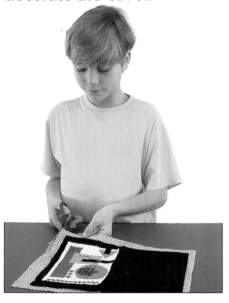

6 Now line the cover. Open out your cover and cut a piece of lining fabric, about half an inch bigger all around.

7 Place the cover on the lining, wrong sides together. Turn over the edge of the lining twice. Sew it to the outside of the cover using tiny hemming stitches.

8 Use a strong thread to stitch through the center folds of the pages and the cover to hold the book together.

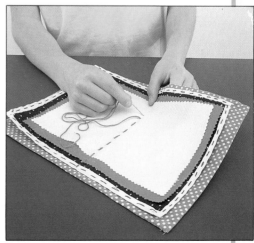

DESIGN IDEAS

Try to find ideas for your work by looking closely at other pieces of sewing, such as clothes, cushions, bags – anything at all. Try to see more than the most obvious features of an item. For example, it is often interesting to look "behind the scenes" at the working parts. In the past, the wrong side of a piece of embroidery, or the hems and **seams** of clothes, although neatly sewn, were hidden away. Now the wrong side is often considered as interesting as the right side.

Try using these forgotten parts of sewing to think up ideas for your own work. Here are some hints.

1 Turn a pair of jeans or a dress inside out. Make some careful drawings of the way the piece of clothing has been put together. Try to use this information in the design of your own embroidery or sewing.

2 Look at the back of a piece of sewing. The marks made by the stitches and the loose ends of thread may suggest abstract patterns and textures.

4 Find some old zippers and take them apart. Sew them onto your work.

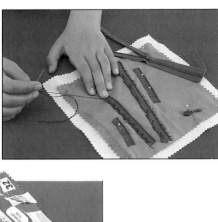

6 Look to see whether the edges have frayed. You may decide not to worry about fraying edges in your own work. Or you may want to make the edges fray more.

3 Look for the labels sewn into store-bought clothes. You could cut out labels from old clothes to use as patches for appliqué work.

5 Look at the ways clothes are fastened. For example, buttonholes can be used to make patterns and add texture to your work.

7 Find a slip or a nightgown that is decorated with pieces of ***broderie anglaise***. Look at the effects of light and shade that can be made by cutting holes in fabric and sewing the edges, and by using white thread on white cloth. See if you can make similar effects in your own work.

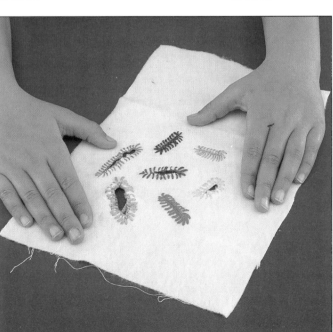

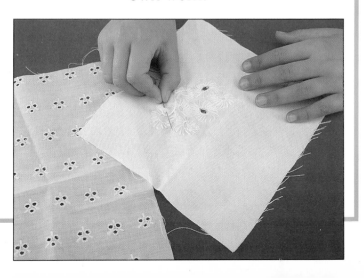

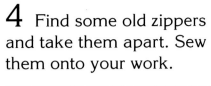

THE GALLERY

Look around you! Look at wildlife and the whole world of nature. Study the buildings and objects made by people. All kinds of things can give you ideas and starting points for sewn and embroidered work. Collect drawings, photographs, and postcards of things that you find exciting and interesting. Take your own photographs. Here are a few pictures to give you some ideas.

Wild grass in the dark ▶

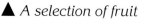 ▲ *A selection of fruit*

An electricity tower ▶

▲ *A hot-air balloon*

▼ *Leopards*

▲ *New York lit up against the night sky*

Beautiful red gerberas ▶

▼ *Children dressed as clowns*

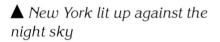

GLOSSARY

Brocades Rich, woven fabrics with a raised design on them.

Broderie anglaise A special kind of embroidery, using white thread on white cotton or linen, which leaves a pattern of small holes in the fabric. The words mean "English embroidery" in French.

Burlap A coarse cloth, like sack material.

Canvas A kind of strong, loosely woven fabric used for embroidery.

Cashmere A very fine, soft wool made from the hair of goats from the area of Kashmir in Pakistan and northern India. Cashmere is an English spelling of Kashmir.

Contrasting Describes things that are very unlike one another.

Diagonal In a slanting direction.

Embroidered Decorated with fancy needlework.

Eye On a sewing needle, the small hole at one end that holds the thread.

Fabric Any kind of cloth made by knitting, weaving, or felting fibers together.

Fibers The threads used to make cloth.

Fray To wear away at the edges.

Grid A network of crisscrossing lines.

Horizontal Going across; the opposite of vertical.

Loom A frame used for weaving cloth. Vertical threads are attached to the loom so that horizontal threads can be woven across them.

Medieval Relating to the Middle Ages, the period of European history from about A.D. 500 to 1500.

Motif A design that is repeated to make a pattern. A motif can also be a theme that runs through a work of art.

Parallel Going in the same direction.

Pattern In sewing, a paper plan of the item being made. The paper shapes are pinned to the fabric and cut around to make the necessary pieces.

Pivoted Attached on a pivot. A pivot is a point on which something turns.

Samplers Pieces of needlepoint made using many different stitches to show the skill of the worker.

Seam The line of stitching that joins two pieces of fabric together.

Societies Groups of people who share the same traditions, history, and way of life.

Swatches Small pieces of cloth used as samples.

Tacking Loose stitching used to hold pieces of fabric together while the permanent stitching is done. The tacking stitches are then removed.

Tailors People who make clothes, particularly men's clothes.

Texture The surface feel of a material.

Vertical Going up and down; the opposite of horizontal.

Wrong side The side of the fabric that will be on the inside of the finished piece. The *right side* will show when the piece is finished.

FURTHER INFORMATION

BOOKS TO READ

Coleman, Anne. *Fabrics and Yarns.* (Vero Beach, FL: Rourke Corporation, 1990).

Lancaster, John. *Fabric Art.* (New York: Franklin Watts, 1991).

Lawler, T. *Sewing and Knitting.* (Tulsa, OK: EDC Publishing, 1979).

Messent, Jan. *Wool 'n Magic: Creative Uses of Yarn.* (Woodstock, NY: Arthur Schwartz & Co., 1989).

O'Reilly, Susie. *Knitting and Crochet.* Arts & Crafts (New York: Thomson Learning, 1994).

Whyman, Kathryn. *Textiles.* Resources Today (New York: Gloucester Press, 1988).

For the left-handed, a simple booklet – *The Left-Hander's Guide to Needlepoint* (published by Left-Handers International) – is available from: Left-Handers International, P.O. Box 8249, Topeka, KS 66608 (tel: 913/234-2177).

For futher information, contact:

The American Craft Council
72 Spring Street
New York, NY 10012

American Sewing Guild
P.O. Box 50976
Indianapolis, IN 46250-0976

American Needlepoint Guild
728 Summerly Drive
Nashville, TN 37209

INDEX

ACKNOWLEDGMENTS

The publishers would like to thank the following for allowing their photographs to be reproduced: American Museum in Britain, Bath © 6 right, 7 top left, 9 bottom; Louise Baldwin 7 bottom right; Crafts Council 4 bottom (James Acord, Susan Shire, Teresa May, and A. Warren); Eye Ubiquitous 4 top, 7 top right (Patrick Bouineau), 28 center right (David Platt), bottom left (David Cumming), and bottom right (Ken Oldroyd); Fitzwilliam Museum, University of Cambridge, The Bridgeman Art Library 7 bottom left; Michael Holford 6 left, 8 center; Images Photo Library 28 bottom left and bottom right, 29 top left and center right; Life File 29 top right (David Heath); Tony Morrison South American Pictures *title* *page*; Walker Art Gallery, Liverpool, The Bridgeman Art Library 8 bottom. All other photographs, including *cover,* were supplied by Zul Mukhida. Logo artwork was supplied by John Yates.

The author would like to thank Ailsa O'Reilly and Ethel Tapp for their advice and help.